Emma Farrarons is a French illustrator and graphic designer. Born on the island of Cebu in the Philippines, Emma grew up in Paris.

She was trained in illustration at the Edinburgh College of Art and l'École nationale supérieure des Arts Décoratifs. Having completed a textile and printmaking course at Capellagården school in Sweden, she has developed a particular love of pattern and fabric print and is inspired by French, Scandinavian and Japanese design. She illustrates and designs books, posters and stationery.

When she is not drawing and designing, Emma enjoys cookery, sewing, travel and practising mindfulness. She lives in London with her Danish husband.

Share your creations using **#mindfulnesscolouringbook**
Visit the Mindfulness Colouring website at
www.mindfulnesscolouring.com
See more of Emma's work at **www.emmafarrarons.com**

Also by Emma Farrarons

The Mindfulness Colouring Book

More Mindfulness Colouring

The Mindfulness Colouring Diary

A to Z of Style by Amy de la Haye,
illustrated by Emma Farrarons

London Colouring Book by Struan Reid,
illustrated by Emma Farrarons

Emma Farrarons

The
MINDFULNESS MOMENTS
COLOURING BOOK

Anti-stress colouring
and activities for busy people

bluebird
books for life

First published 2016 by Boxtree

This edition published 2021 by Bluebird
an imprint of Pan Macmillan
The Smithson, 6 Briset Street, London EC1M 5NR
Associated companies throughout the world
www.panmacmillan.com

ISBN 978-1-5290-6422-3

Pan Macmillan does not have any control over, or any responsibility for,
any author or third-party websites referred to in or on this book.

1 3 5 7 9 8 6 4 2

A CIP catalogue record for this book is available from the British Library.

Printed in Italy

Visit **www.panmacmillan.com** to read more about all our books
and to buy them. You will also find features, author interviews and
news of any author events, and you can sign up for e-newsletters
so that you're always first to hear about our new releases.

For Viggo Bruun Farrarons

INTRODUCTION

In a stressed-out world, mindfulness has been hailed as a tonic for busy modern living. By clearing our minds and allowing our thoughts, feelings and bodies to simply exist in the moment, we can enjoy sweet moments of peace and calm. Pretty much any activity, done right, can be a mindfulness activity, but colouring in – the act of carefully and attentively filling a page with colour – is particularly suited to mindful meditation.

The 'Mindfulness Colouring' series, with its beautiful templates for colour and creativity, has already helped a million people worldwide to feel calmer and more at peace. *Mindfulness Moments* is a colouring book that offers more stunning illustrations, elegant patterns and tranquil scenes from designer and illustrator Emma Farrarons. Peppered throughout these pages, you will also find simple and imaginative activities to make your days more mindful.

Wherever you go, take this book with you and colour, create and play. It only takes a few moments to feel better and we hope this book will give you lots of ideas for how to live a calmer life.

Emma Farrarons

Choose a fruit for this exercise – a clementine would work well. Hold it in your hand. Observe the colour, the weight in your palm, the shape. Inhale the scent of the skin and also how the light reflects off it. Does it feel cool in your hand? Peel back the skin and witness the fine mist of juice that is released. Note the sensation of the skin as it breaks under your nail. How does the fruit smell now? Pay attention to the shapes you make with the skin as you peel it off. What sound do you notice as you separate each segment? Put a segment in your mouth. Note the coolness of the fruit as it touches your tongue. Take a bite and chew slowly. How does the clementine taste? Can you identify the different flavours on your tongue? Is it sweet, sour, bitter?

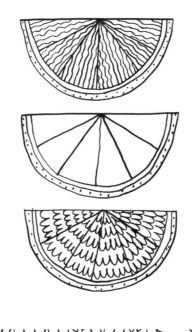

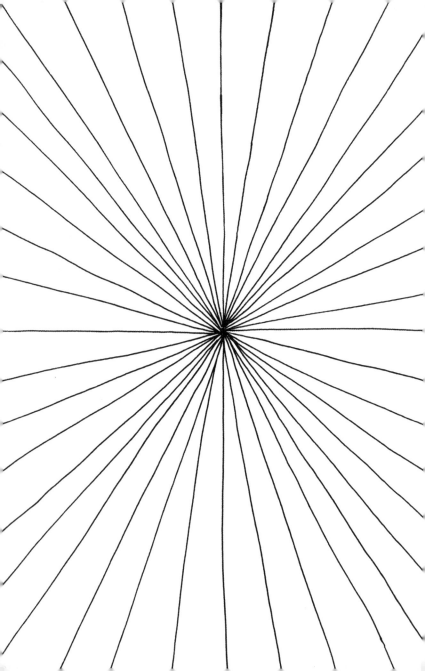

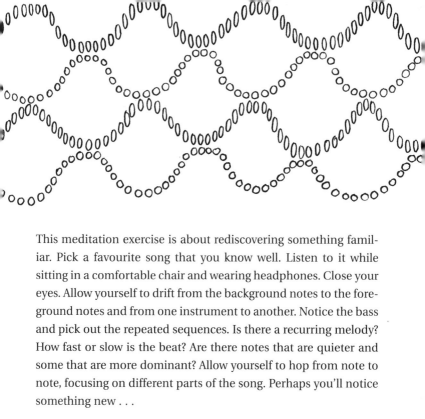

This meditation exercise is about rediscovering something familiar. Pick a favourite song that you know well. Listen to it while sitting in a comfortable chair and wearing headphones. Close your eyes. Allow yourself to drift from the background notes to the foreground notes and from one instrument to another. Notice the bass and pick out the repeated sequences. Is there a recurring melody? How fast or slow is the beat? Are there notes that are quieter and some that are more dominant? Allow yourself to hop from note to note, focusing on different parts of the song. Perhaps you'll notice something new . . .

Create your own paper snowflake. Fold your paper as shown here and mindfully cut out shapes at random. Don't cut all the way across. Notice the feel of the paper and the sound it makes as you fold it. Bring your attention to the shapes you cut out. Unfold and reveal your mindful creation.

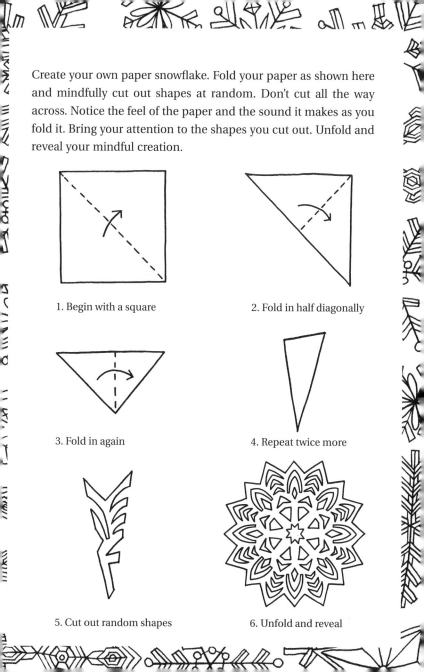

1. Begin with a square

2. Fold in half diagonally

3. Fold in again

4. Repeat twice more

5. Cut out random shapes

6. Unfold and reveal

Fill this image with warm colours such as burnt orange, ochre, lemon yellow, fuchsia, rose pink, nut brown, brick red, saffron, maroon, burgundy or apricot. If you don't have a wide variety of colours in your pencil case, then blend shades together to create new colours.

Decorate your own egg cup! You will need a wooden egg cup and some acrylic paint. If you can't get hold of an egg cup, try painting the eggshell itself.

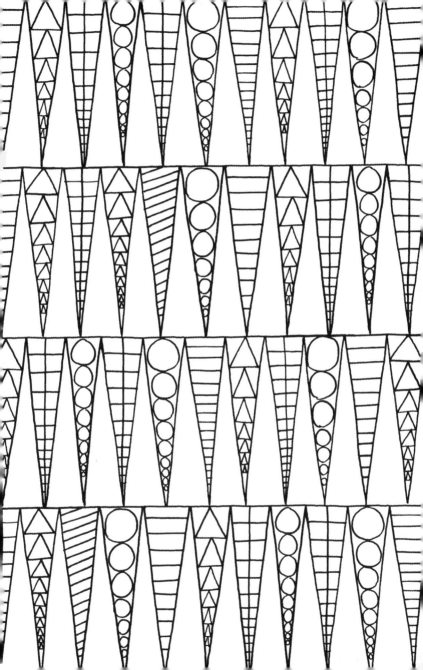

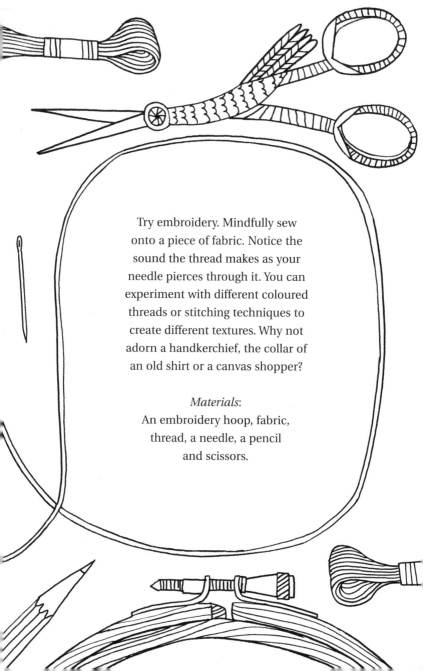

Try embroidery. Mindfully sew onto a piece of fabric. Notice the sound the thread makes as your needle pierces through it. You can experiment with different coloured threads or stitching techniques to create different textures. Why not adorn a handkerchief, the collar of an old shirt or a canvas shopper?

Materials:
An embroidery hoop, fabric, thread, a needle, a pencil and scissors.

Here are simple embroidery templates that you can use for inspiration. Trace onto fabric and sew over the lines.

Draw and colour in your own flower mandala.
Use these illustrated leaves and petals for inspiration.

You can also make a flower mandala with real petals and leaves.

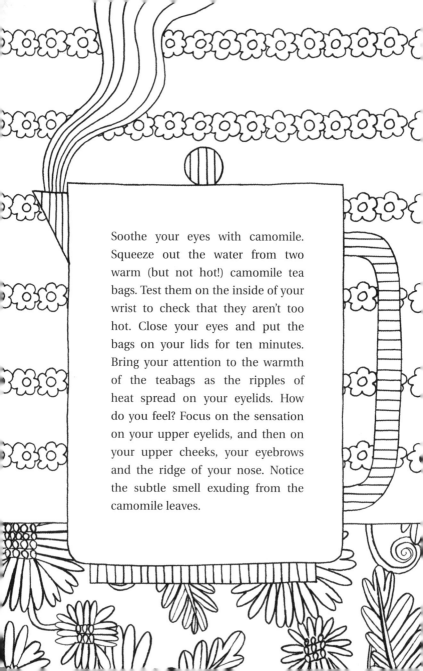

Soothe your eyes with camomile. Squeeze out the water from two warm (but not hot!) camomile tea bags. Test them on the inside of your wrist to check that they aren't too hot. Close your eyes and put the bags on your lids for ten minutes. Bring your attention to the warmth of the teabags as the ripples of heat spread on your eyelids. How do you feel? Focus on the sensation on your upper eyelids, and then on your upper cheeks, your eyebrows and the ridge of your nose. Notice the subtle smell exuding from the camomile leaves.

Find a place with an interesting view. A cafe on a street corner with large windows would work well. Sit down, order a drink and observe what is going on in front of your eyes. Write down everything that you see. The more you describe, the more visual your writing will become.

_____

_____

_____

_____

_____

_____

_____

_____

_____

_____

_____

_____

_____

_____

_____

_____

_____

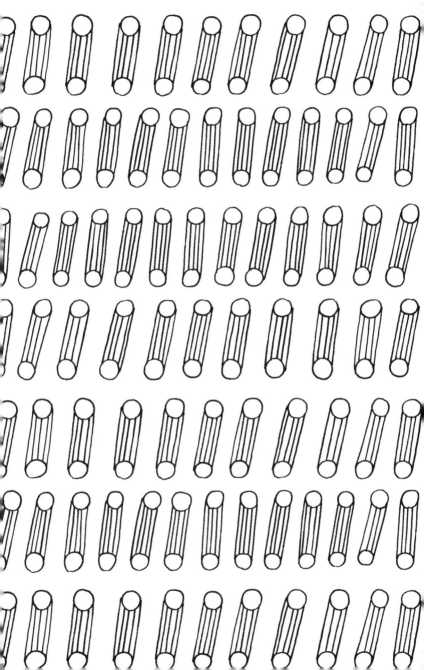

Banana skins have a very satisfying texture to draw on.
With a ball point pen, mindfully draw a pattern onto the skin
with no particular design in mind.

Notice how the pen smoothly rolls on the banana skin and
observe the pattern that you're forming. If you prefer to paint
then you could try this exercise on a pebble.

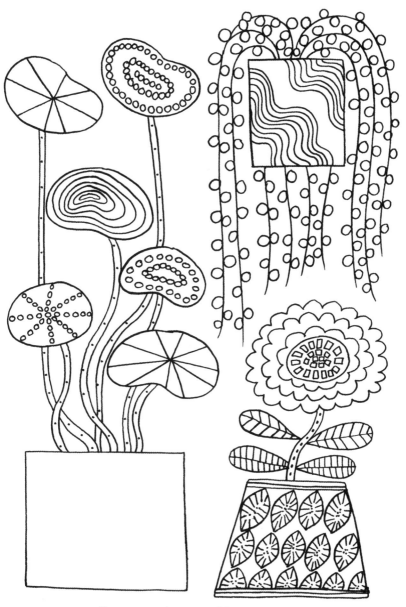

Decorate a plant pot with a pattern.

Mindfully draw a henna pattern on this palm. You can also trace
your hand onto paper and create more henna patterns.

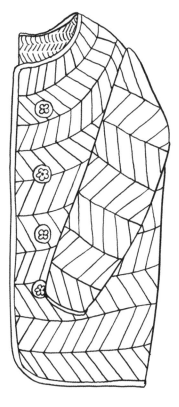

This exercise is about turning something mundane into something mindful. Ironing a shirt, for example. Notice the crumples as they turn smooth underneath the hot iron. Hear the gurgling sound of the water in the iron and the hiss of steam evaporating in the air. What can you smell?

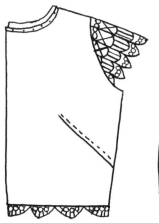

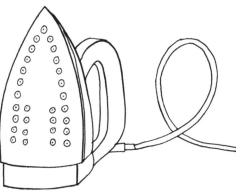

This tree needs foliage.
Can you mindfully draw
different shaped leaves?

This exercise is about taking note of, and being mindful of, the world around you.

Stand in the rain without an umbrella.

Does your street look, sound or smell different?

Notice the sensation of the droplets of water as they touch your skin, the sound they make as they hit the floor and the ripples in the puddles.

Take one avocado seed.

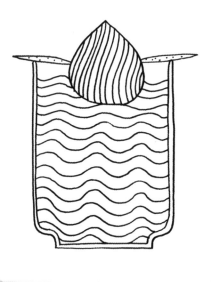

Use four toothpicks to pierce the sides of the seed so that you can securely balance it on a glass.

Half submerge the seed in water. Check on it every day.

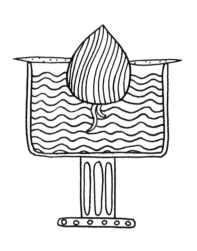

In time, you will notice roots sprouting from it. The seed is now ready for planting.

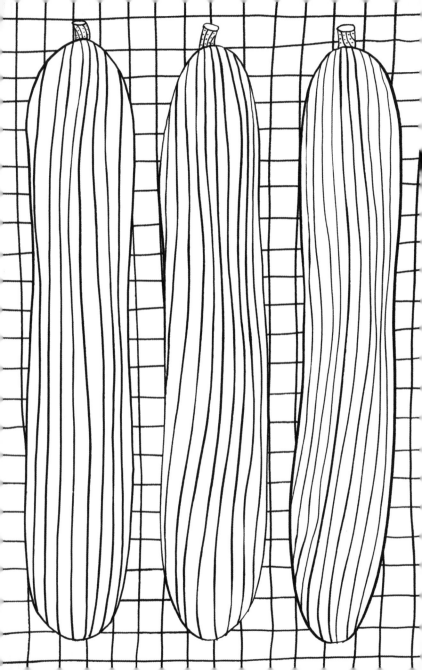

Find a quiet time of the day to do this meditation. Cut two slices of well-chilled cucumber. Lie down on a comfortable but firm, flat surface. Close your eyes and place the cucumber onto your lids. Keep still, with your arms by your sides and your palms facing down. Notice the sensation of the cucumber slices as they come into contact with your eyelids. Do they feel cool? What do they smell like? Notice the wetness on your skin as the slices touch the ridge of your nose, your eyebrows and upper cheekbones. If you become distracted by your thoughts, don't worry – just bring your attention back to the cucumbers. Then sit up and take a few deep breaths. How do you feel now?

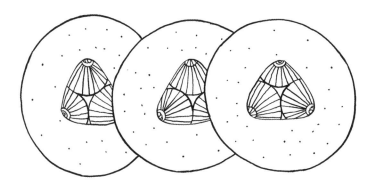

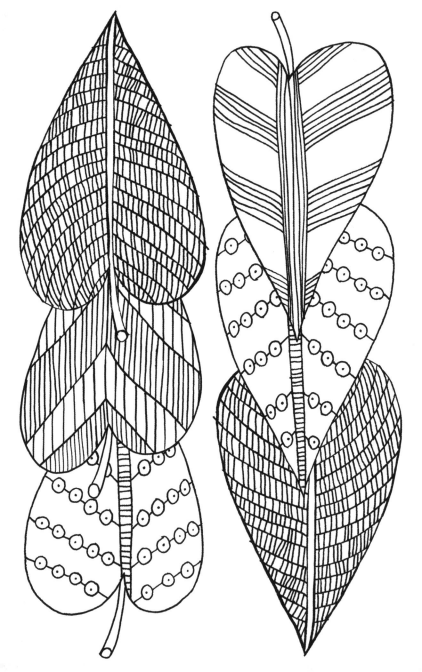

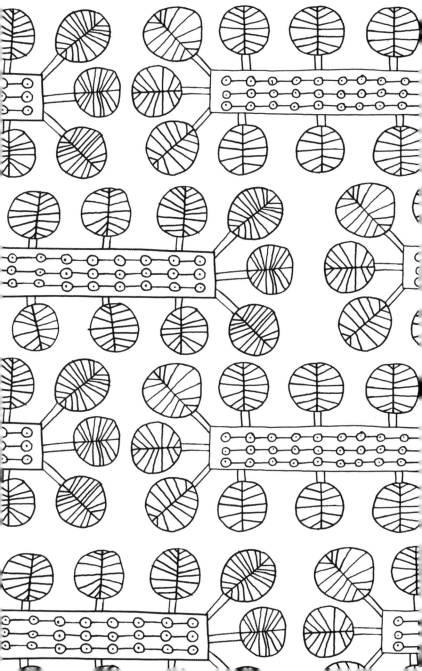

Complete the grid with your own patterns.

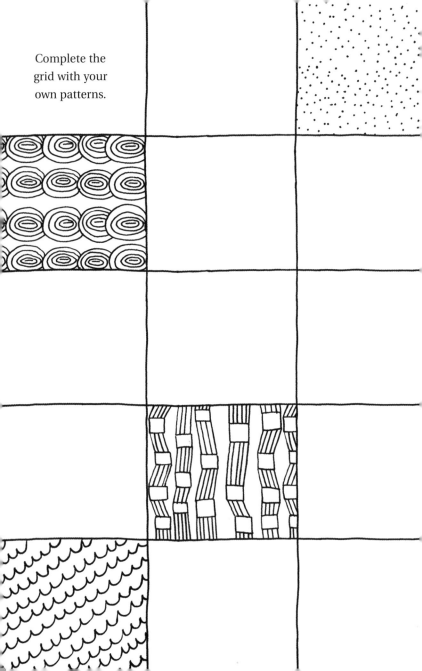

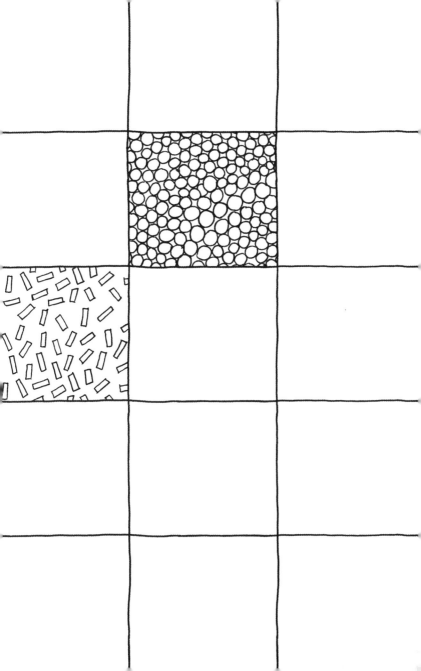

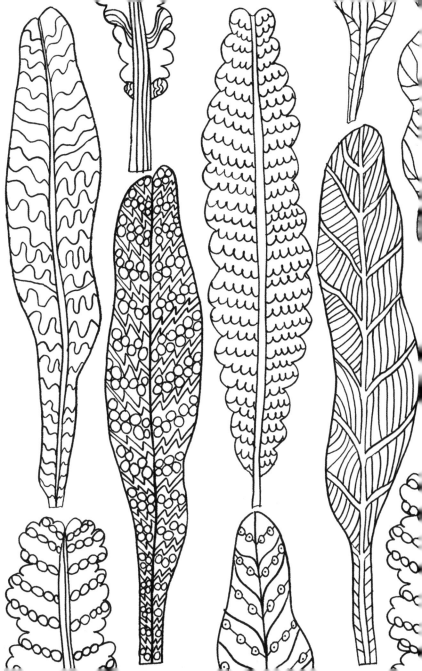

Write down a list of foods that you wish to mindfully taste:

☐ dark chocolate 🍫   ☐
☐ an apple 🍎   ☐
☐   ☐
☐   ☐
☐   ☐
☐   ☐
☐   ☐
☐   ☐
☐   ☐
☐   ☐
☐   ☐
☐   ☐
☐   ☐
☐   ☐
☐   ☐
☐   ☐
☐   ☐

Break your morning routine . . .

Change your journey to work.

Leave earlier to allow time for exploring.

Walk along a different street.

Get your morning drink from a different coffee shop.

Did you notice something new?

Take a break from whatever you are doing to carry out a simple neck stretch. Rest your right hand on your crown and tilt your head to the right. Hold the pose. Breathe slowly in and out. Notice the gentle warmth on your muscles as they soften and stretch. Bring awareness to the weight of your hand on your head. Straighten your neck back to a neutral position and repeat on the left side.

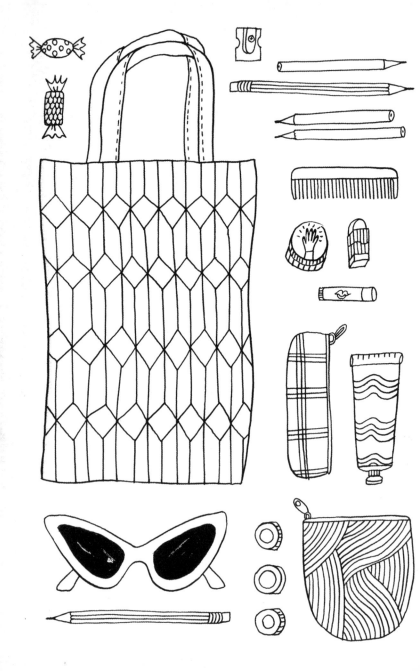

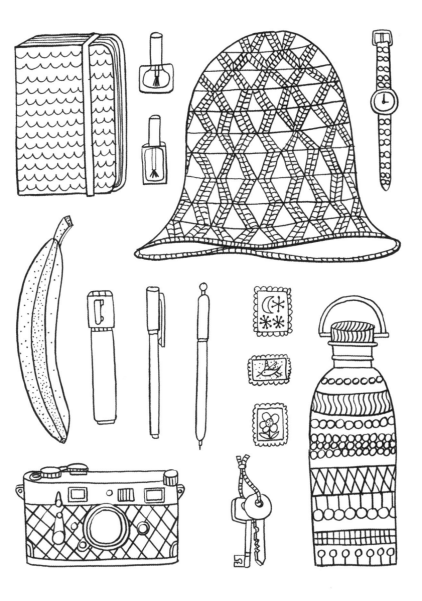

Give your wallet or bag a tidy. Take everything out, clean it and then put everything back in.

Fill this painter's palette with colour.

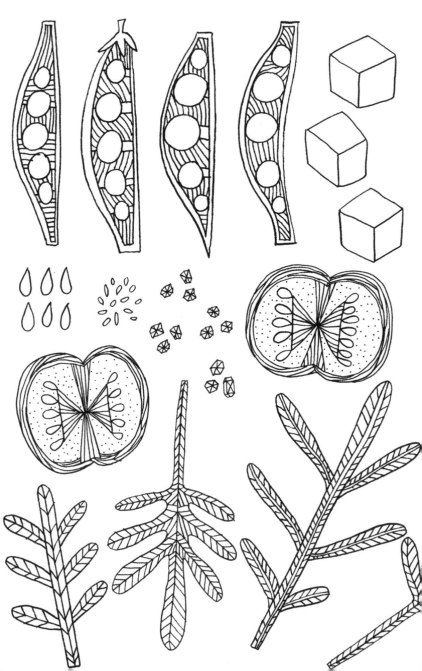

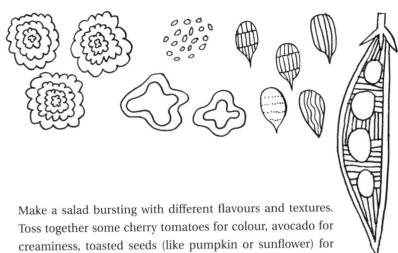

Make a salad bursting with different flavours and textures. Toss together some cherry tomatoes for colour, avocado for creaminess, toasted seeds (like pumpkin or sunflower) for texture, sugar snap peas for crunch and sweetness, rocket leaves for a peppery kick, chopped parsley for freshness and crumbled feta for tanginess. Experiment with quantities and dress with rock salt, balsamic vinegar and extra-virgin olive oil. Practise mindful tasting.

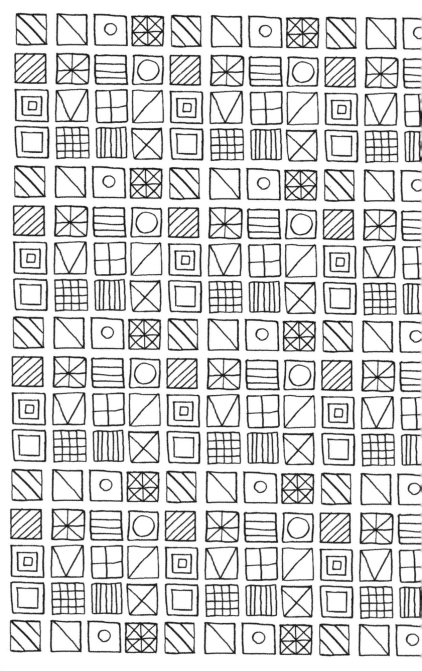

Try colouring in using only cool colours – greens, blues and purples such as ice-blue, aqua, indigo, cobalt, duck egg, teal, turquoise, cerulean, sapphire, emerald, aubergine, amethyst and grey.

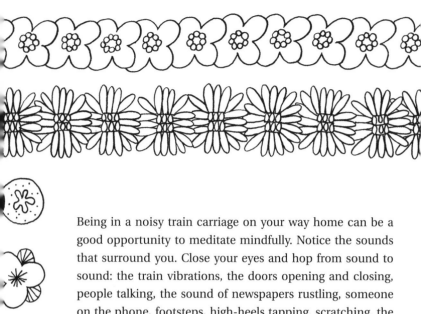

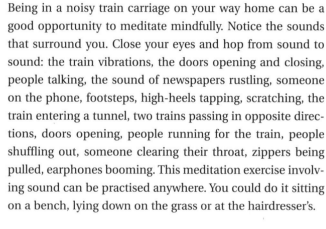

Being in a noisy train carriage on your way home can be a good opportunity to meditate mindfully. Notice the sounds that surround you. Close your eyes and hop from sound to sound: the train vibrations, the doors opening and closing, people talking, the sound of newspapers rustling, someone on the phone, footsteps, high-heels tapping, scratching, the train entering a tunnel, two trains passing in opposite directions, doors opening, people running for the train, people shuffling out, someone clearing their throat, zippers being pulled, earphones booming. This meditation exercise involving sound can be practised anywhere. You could do it sitting on a bench, lying down on the grass or at the hairdresser's.

Go into a comfortable room – your living room for example – just before dusk. Make sure your curtains and windows are open. Sit in a cozy chair and take note of how the daylight falls on the objects around you. When the sun has gone down and it is almost dark, light a candle and turn off the lights. Notice how the flames brighten the room as they flicker in the darkness. Bring attention to how your mood changes when you do this. Do you feel relaxed?

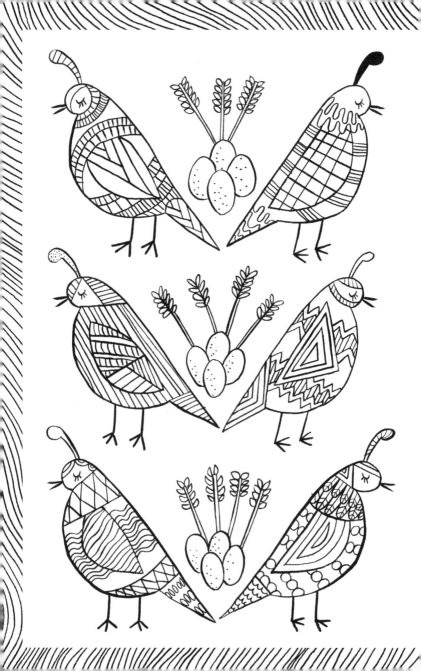

Turn off your phone and other electronic devices for an hour or more. Spend some time away from digital updates.

Make room in your busy
schedule for some mind-
fulness moments.

MONDAY

TUESDAY

WEDNESDAY

THURSDAY

FRIDAY

SATURDAY

SUNDAY

Create a mindfulness chatterbox filled with eight different mindfulness activities. Fold a square piece of paper as shown here. You can use the template below as a guide.

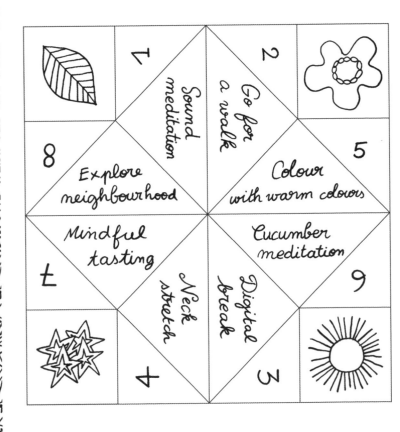

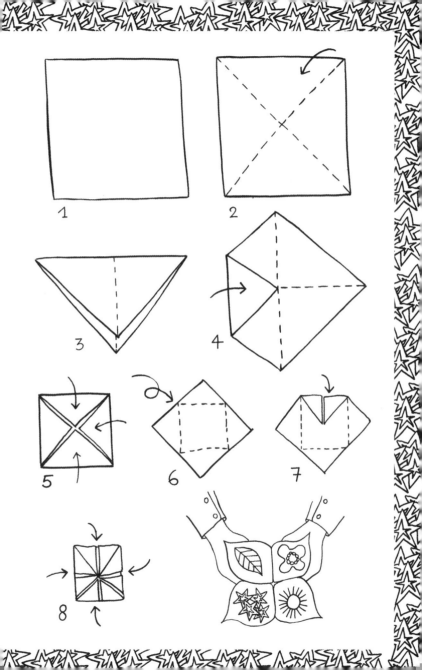

1

2

3

4

5

6

7

8

THANKS

Tusind tak to Mette and Nils. Have you spotted the kale
from your garden?

And thank you to my mindful colouring friends
around the world.

EMMA FARRARONS
illustration & art direction

www.emmafarrarons.com